Southern Elephant Seal

The Biggest Seal in the World

by Meish Goldish

Consultant: Jenny Montague
Assistant Curator of Marine Mammals
New England Aquarium
Boston, MA

BEARPORT
PUBLISHING

New York, New York

Credits

Cover, © Momatiuk-Eastcott/Corbis; TOC, © James Richey/iStockphoto; 4, Kathrin Ayer; 4–5, © Yva Momatiuk & John Eastcott/Corbis; 6T, © Tom Ulrich/Visuals Unlimited, Inc.; 6B, © Martin Vrlik/Shutterstock; 7, © Peter Bassett/NPL/Minden Pictures; 8, © Yva Momatiuk & John Eastcott/Minden Pictures; 9, © James Richey/iStockphoto; 10, © Don Paulson Photography/SuperStock; 11, © Francisco Erize/Bruce Coleman/Photoshot; 12, © David Wrobel/Visuals Unlimited, Inc.; 13, © D. Parer & E. Parer-Cook/Auscape/Minden Pictures; 14, © Yva Momatiuk & John Eastcott/Minden Pictures; 15, © Fred Bruemmer/DRK Photo; 16, © Don Paulson Photography/SuperStock; 17, © Pete Oxford/Nature Picture Library; 18, © Yva Momatiuk & John Eastcott/Minden Pictures; 19, © Yva Momatiuk & John Eastcott/Minden Pictures; 20, © Peter Scoones/NPL/Minden Pictures; 21, © Yva Momatiuk & John Eastcott/Minden Pictures; 22L, © Age Fotostock/SuperStock; 22C, © Richard Sidey/iStockphoto; 22R, © Darren Begley/Shutterstock; 23TL, © Francisco Erize/Bruce Coleman/Photoshot; 23TR, © Yva Momatiuk & John Eastcott/Minden Pictures; 23BL, © Peter Scoones/NPL/Minden Pictures; 23BR, © David Wrobel/Visuals Unlimited, Inc.; 23BKG, © Pablo H Caridad/Shutterstock.

Publisher: Kenn Goin
Senior Editor: Lisa Wiseman
Creative Director: Spencer Brinker
Original Design: Otto Carbajal
Photo Researcher: Picture Perfect Professionals, LLC

Library of Congress Cataloging-in-Publication Data

Goldish, Meish.
  Southern elephant seal : the biggest seal in the world / by Meish Goldish ; consultant, Jenny Montague.
      p. cm. — (More supersized!)
  Includes bibliographical references and index.
  ISBN-13: 978-1-936087-26-6 (library binding)
  ISBN-10: 1-936087-26-X (library binding)
  1. Southern elephant seal—Juvenile literature. I. Title.
  QL737.P64G65 2010
  599.79′4—dc22
                                2009028301

For more information, write to Bearport Publishing Company, Inc., 101 Fifth Avenue, Suite 6R, New York, New York 10003. Printed in the United States of America in North Mankato, Minnesota.

102009
090309CGA

10 9 8 7 6 5 4 3 2 1

Contents

Big and Heavy

The southern elephant seal is the biggest seal in the world.

With its head raised, an adult male southern elephant seal is taller than an adult human.

Male southern elephant seals can grow to be up to 21 feet (6.4 m) long and weigh more than 8,000 pounds (3,629 kg). Females can grow to be 10 feet (3 m) long and weigh 2,000 pounds (907 kg).

What's in a Name?

Southern elephant seals got their name because the male seals have noses that when filled with air look like elephant trunks.

The seals look like elephants in other ways, too.

Both animals are large.

Also, many of these seals, like elephants, are gray.

Southern elephant seals are also called "sea elephants."

a male elephant seal's nose

an elephant's trunk

male elephant seal

Home in the Sea

Southern elephant seals live in the freezing waters near Antarctica.

They spend nearly all their time there.

Some of the few times they go on land are to mate and to have babies.

Southern elephant seals are related to northern elephant seals, which live in the northern part of the world in the Pacific Ocean.

male elephant seal

back flippers

front flipper

Finding Food

Southern elephant seals hunt for food in the ocean.

They dive deep down to find fish and **squid**.

While hunting, the seals have to watch out for big sharks and killer whales that want to eat them.

Southern elephant seals can dive as deep as one mile (1.6 km) down in the ocean. They can stay underwater for up to two hours without coming up for air.

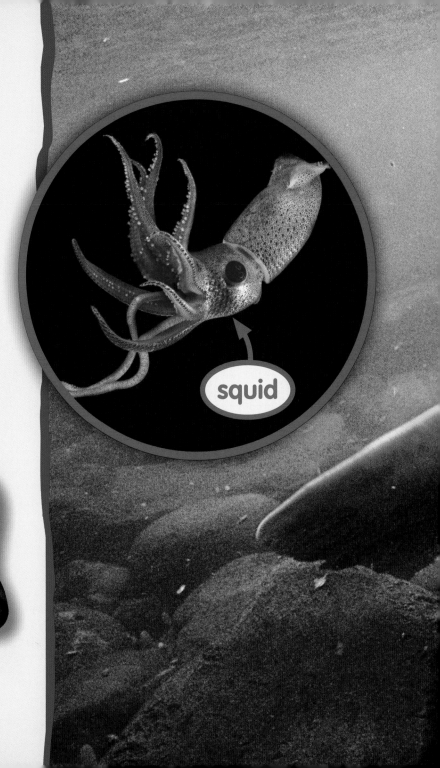

squid

Life on Land

Every spring, southern elephant seals swim more than 1,000 miles (1,609 km) to reach a place on land to mate.

When the seals come ashore, the area where they gather is called a **rookery**.

There, the males fight with one another to see who will mate with the females.

The females will give birth one year after mating.

rookery

Male southern elephant seals roar loudly when they fight one another. The roaring can be heard more than one mile (1.6 km) away.

15

Old and New

Three weeks after mating, the adult southern elephant seals leave their rookery and return to the ocean.

They stay there for about three months.

In the summer, they swim back to land, where their skin and hair fall off their bodies.

Within a month, the seals grow new skin and hair that gives them an extra layer of warmth.

Then they return to the ocean once again and stay there throughout the winter.

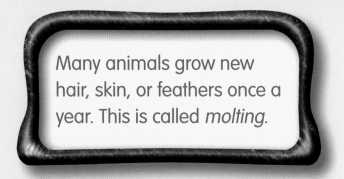

Many animals grow new hair, skin, or feathers once a year. This is called *molting*.

skin before molting

17

Having a Baby

As spring approaches, the adult males return to the rookery.

About one to three weeks later, the adult female southern elephant seals return to give birth.

Each female has one baby seal, called a **pup**.

The pup drinks its mother's milk for about three weeks.

Then the adults go back to the ocean, and the pup is left on its own.

pup

A southern elephant seal pup weighs about 100 pounds (45 kg) at birth. A month later, the pup may weigh as much as 500 pounds (227 kg)!

Growing Up

A southern elephant seal pup stays on land for about two months.

Then it goes into the ocean for the first time, where it learns to swim and hunt on its own.

It keeps on growing, too.

By the age of five, it's ready to start its own family of giant seals.

Southern elephant seals can live for about 23 years. Today, there are about 600,000 southern elephant seals in the world.

More Big Mammals

Southern elephant seals belong to a group of animals called mammals. Almost all mammals give birth to live young. The babies drink milk from their mothers. Mammals are also warm-blooded and have hair or fur on their skin.

Here are three more big seals.

Northern Elephant Seal

The northern elephant seal can weigh up to 4,500 pounds (2,041 kg).

Weddell Seal

The Weddell seal can weigh up to 1,200 pounds (544 kg).

Leopard Seal

The leopard seal can reach a weight of 1,000 pounds (454 kg).

Southern Elephant Seal:
8,000 pounds/3,629 kg

Northern Elephant Seal:
4,500 pounds/2,014 kg

Weddell Seal:
1,200 pounds/544 kg

Leopard Seal:
1,000 pounds/454 kg

Glossary

flippers (FLIP-urz) short, webbed, wing-like body parts; the front flippers are used for steering while the back flippers are used to help the seal move faster

rookery (RUK-ur-ee) a place where large numbers of southern elephant seals gather to mate

pup (PUHP) a young seal

squid (SKWID) a sea animal with a long, soft body and ten arm-like body parts

23

Index

Read More

Gray, Susan Heinrichs. *Elephant Seal.* Ann Arbor, MI: Cherry Lake (2007).

Kalman, Bobbie. *Seals and Sea Lions.* New York: Crabtree Publishing (2005).

Lynch, Wayne. *Seals.* Minnetonka, MN: NorthWord Books (2002).

Learn More Online

To learn more about southern elephant seals, visit
www.bearportpublishing.com/MoreSuperSized